Primary Sources in World History

THE MODERN AGE

ENZO GEORGE

Cavendish
Square
New York

Published in 2017 by Cavendish Square Publishing, LLC
243 5th Avenue, Suite 136 New York, NY 10016

© 2017 Brown Bear Books Ltd

Website: cavendishsq.com

This publication represents the opinions and views of the author based on his or her personal experiences, knowledge, and research. The information in this book serves as a general guide only. The author and publisher have used their best efforts in preparing this book and disclaim liabilty rising directly or indirectly for the use and application of this book.

CPSIA compliance information: Batch #CS16CSQ.

All websites were available and accurate when this book went to press.

Library of Congress Cataloging-in-Publication Data

Names: George, Enzo.
Title: The Modern Age / Enzo George.
Description: New York : Cavendish Square, 2017. | Series: Primary sources in world history | Includes index.
Identifiers: ISBN 9781502618283 (library bound) | ISBN 9781502618290 (ebook)
Subjects: LCSH: History, Modern—20th century—Juvenile literature.
Classification: LCC D421.G47 2017 | DDC 909.82—dc23

For Brown Bear Books Ltd:
Editorial Director: Lindsey Lowe
Managing Editor: Tim Cooke
Children's Publisher: Anne O'Daly
Design Manager: Keith Davis
Designer: Lynne Lennon
Picture Manager: Sophie Mortimer

Picture Credits:
Front Cover: Getty Images: Stuart Macgladrie /Sydney Morning Herald/Fairfax Media main; Shutterstock: ilolab map.
Interior: Dreamstime: Gepapix 21; Government Press Office: 30; Hindustan Times: 27; Library of Congress: 8, 12, 13, 14, 19, 24, 29, 36; NARA: 33, 38, 39, 40; Oakland Public Library: Edward A. "Doc" Rogers 15; Robert Hunt Library: 6, 7, 9, 10, 16, 17, 20, 22, 23, 25, 26, 28, 31, 32, 34, 37, IWM 11; Ronald Reagan Library: 41; Shutterstock: Anthony Correia 42; Topfoto: The Granger Collection 35, Topham Picturepoint 18; US Army: DOD/Christopher S. Barnhart 43.

Brown Bear Books has made every attempt to contact the copyright holder.
If you have any information please contact licensing@brownbearbooks.co.uk

We believe the extracts included in this book to be material in the public domain.
Anyone having further information should contact licensing@brownbearbooks.co.uk

Printed in the United States of America

CONTENTS

INTRODUCTION

Primary sources are the best way to get close to people from the past. They include the things people wrote in diaries, letters, or books; the paintings, drawings, maps, or cartoons they created; and even the buildings they constructed, the clothes they wore, or the objects they owned. Such sources often reveal a lot about how people saw themselves and how they thought about their world.

This book collects a range of primary sources in world history from World War I (1914–1918) until the early twenty-first century. The period was one of great political, technological, and social change that shaped the world in which we live.

World War I was the first truly global conflict, and its consequences shaped much of the first half of the twentieth century. The war left Europe's economy in ruins, while a revolution in Russia created a state dedicated to spreading communism around the world. Political extremism grew and ultimately led to the outbreak of World War II (1939–1945). That conflict also had lasting consequences. European countries could no longer afford to maintain colonies in Africa and Asia, and new independent countries emerged. Meanwhile the so-called Cold War divided the globe into free world and communist regions for nearly fifty years of international tension.

HOW TO USE THIS BOOK

Each spread contains at least one primary source. Look out for "Source Explored" boxes that explain images from the modern world and who made them and why. There are also "As They Saw It" boxes that contain quotes from people of the period.

Some boxes contain more detailed information about a particular aspect of a subject. The subjects are arranged in roughly chronological order. They focus on key events or people. There is a full timeline of the period at the back of the book.

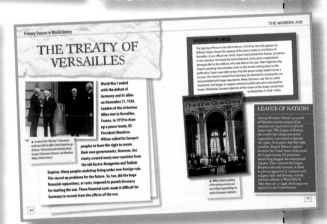

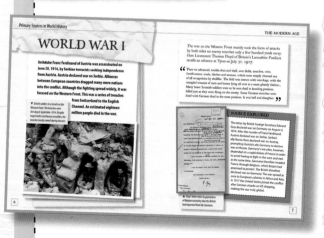

Some spreads feature a longer extract from a contemporary eyewitness. Look for the colored introduction that explains who the writer is and the origin of his or her account. These accounts are often accompanied by a related visual primary source.

WORLD WAR I

Archduke Franz Ferdinand of Austria was assassinated on June 28, 1914, by Serbian terrorists seeking independence from Austria. Austria declared war on Serbia. Alliances between European countries meant that many more nations joined the conflict. Although the fighting spread around the world, it was focused on the Western Front. This was a series of trenches from Switzerland to the English Channel. An estimated eighteen million people died in the war.

▼ British soldiers in a trench on the Western Front. The trenches were first dug in September 1914. Despite huge battles and heavy casualties, the trenches barely moved during the war.

The war on the Western Front mainly took the form of attacks by both sides on enemy trenches only a few hundred yards away. Here Lieutenant Thomas Floyd of Britain's Lancashire Fusiliers recalls an advance at Ypres on July 31, 1917:

66 Thus we advanced, amidst shot and shell, over fields, trenches, wire, fortifications, roads, ditches and streams, which were simply churned out of all recognition by shellfire. The field was strewn with wreckage, with the mangled remains of men and horses lying all over in a most ghastly fashion... Many brave Scottish soldiers were to be seen dead in kneeling position, killed just as they were firing on the enemy. Some German trenches were lined with German dead in the same position. It was hell and slaughter. **99**

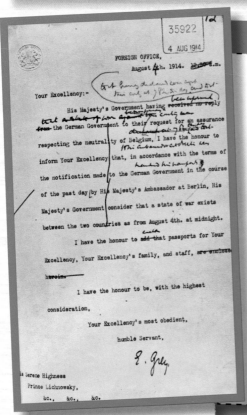

▲ Gray's letter refers to guarantees of Belgian neutrality that the British had requested from the Germans.

SOURCE EXPLORED

This letter by British Foreign Secretary Edward Gray declared war on Germany on August 4, 1914. After the murder of Franz Ferdinand, Austria declared war on Serbia. Serbia's ally Russia then declared war on Austria, prompting Austria's ally Germany to declare war on Russia. Germany's war plan, however, depended on a rapid defeat of France in order to avoid having to fight in the west and east at the same time. Germany therefore invaded France through Belgium, which Britain had promised to protect. The British therefore declared war on Germany. The war spread at once to European colonies in Africa and Asia. In 1917 the United States joined the conflict after German attacks on US shipping, making the war truly global.

THE RUSSIAN REVOLUTION

Revolutionary soldiers in St. Petersburg, then the capital of Russia. Many revolutionaries were military veterans.

Russia had been ruled by the Romanov family since 1613. During World War I, however, defeats by Germany and huge Russian casualties led to social unrest. The Russian Revolution that followed was really two events. In February 1917, the Russian parliament set up a provisional government and the ruler, Czar Nicolas, abdicated. Nicolas and his family were later murdered. In November 1917 (October in the traditional calendar), communists seized power. They set up councils of workers and soldiers, called soviets, to run cities. Led by Vladimir Lenin, the most extreme communists—called the Bolsheviks—came to rule Russia.

▼ *The red flag that appears in this poster became one of the international symbols of communism.*

ПОД ЗНАМЕНЕМ ЛЕНИНА —
ВПЕРЕД К МИРОВОМУ ОКТЯБРЮ!

AS THEY SAW IT

" When Lenin said that Communism is Soviet power plus electrification, I decided that I should become an electrical engineer, that that was my holy duty ... And I didn't want to just draw up plans. I wanted to build an electric power station. That was my mission and I achieved it ... The revolution gave me the right to feel equal to any man. It gave me the right to work, to study what I wanted to study. "

—Ella Shistyer, a student in Russia in 1923, recalls the inspiration of Lenin.

SOURCE EXPLORED

This poster shows the Bolshevik leader, Vladimir Lenin, pointing to the future above the slogan, "Under the banner, forward to the world October!"—calling for the October Revolution to be repeated around the world. The foot of the poster illustrates revolutionaries from across the globe. Propaganda posters helped spread the communist message at a time when most Russians were illiterate. The image presents Lenin as a paternal, kindly figure. In fact, he ruled as a dictator, crushing those who disagreed with him. After the Revolution, Russia descended into civil war and famine as the communists, or Reds, defeated the White Russians who rejected communism. In 1922, Lenin created the Soviet Union to replace Russia. When he died in 1924, Joseph Stalin became Soviet leader and continued the dictatorship.

THE TREATY OF VERSAILLES

▲ *Leaders of the "Big Four" at the peace conference* (left to right): *David Lloyd George (Britain), Vittorio Emanuele Orlando (Italy), Georges Clemenceau (France), and Woodrow Wilson (United States).*

World War I ended with the defeat of Germany and its allies on November 11, 1918. Leaders of the victorious Allies met in Versailles, France, in 1919 to draw up a peace treaty. US President Woodrow Wilson called for Europe's peoples to have the right to create their own governments. However, the treaty created many new countries from the old Austro-Hungarian and Turkish Empires. Many peoples ended up living under new foreign rule. This stored up problems for the future. So, too, did the huge financial reparations, or costs, imposed to punish Germany for starting the war. These financial costs made it difficult for Germany to recover from the effects of the war.

SOURCE EXPLORED

The Signing of Peace in the Hall of Mirrors (1919) by the Irish painter Sir William Orpen shows the signing of the peace treaty in the Palace of Versailles. As an official war artist, Orpen had painted the horrors of warfare in the trenches. He found the bad-tempered, petty peace negotations disrespectful to the millions who had died in the war. That might be why Orpen's painting concentrates more on the ornate setting than on the politicians. Orpen was right to fear that the peace treaty would not be a success. The French insisted that Germany be blamed for starting the war and punished with huge reparations. Many Germans saw this as unfair treatment, and began to support extremist politicians who criticized the treaty. Ultimately, German rejection of the terms of the treaty would lead to World War II (1939–1945).

▲ William Orpen's painting of the signing ceremony was one of three large paintings he made of the peace conference.

LEAGUE OF NATIONS

Among Woodrow Wilson's proposals at Versailles was the creation of an international organization to prevent future wars. This League of Nations, the world's first intergovernmental organization, was created on January 10, 1920. At its peak it had fifty-eight members. Despite Wilson's support, however, the United States never joined the League because US politicians feared being dragged into international disputes. That weakened the League. Despite some early successes, it failed to prevent aggression by countries such as Japan, Italy, and Germany, and the eventual outbreak of World War II. After that war, in 1946, the League was replaced by the United Nations.

SUFFRAGISTS

▲ *An American suffragist campaigns for male support in 1914. Many men were hostile toward the idea of allowing women to vote in elections.*

In 1900 women were unable to vote in national elections in Europe and North America. In Britain and the United States, women campaigned for the vote, or suffrage. These suffragists, or suffragettes, held meetings and parades to try to persuade male politicians to support their cause. During World War I, women in both countries did vital work, such as making weapons in factories. Women's sacrifices in the war convinced governments to give women the vote. British women aged over thirty got the vote in 1918. In the United States, the Nineteenth Amendment gave women the vote in August 1920.

SOURCE EXPLORED

This magazine cover from June 1873 is entitled "The Woman Who Dared." It shows the leading suffragist, Susan B. Anthony, wearing a top hat and spurs. Behind her is a policewoman while at right two men hold a baby and food, reversing the usual roles of men and women. In the background is a parade demanding female suffrage. Anthony became one of the leaders of the suffrage movement after attending the Seneca Falls Convention in July 1848. The two-day convention in Upstate New York produced the first organized call for women to be allowed to vote when it issued the "Declaration of Sentiments." The convention placed the issue of suffrage at the heart of the campaign for increased rights for American women.

▲ *This edition of the Daily Graphic was published on June 5, 1873.*

Up to eight thousand suffragists who paraded through Washington, DC, on March 3, 1913, faced taunts and insults from crowds of bystanders. Here, one of the marchers describes her experience to a Senate committee shortly afterward:

❝ There was no space whatsoever. There was not 10 inches between us and the crowd. I had with me a number of young girls in our division—my daughter and one or two others—and the crowd did hoot and jeer and make the most insulting remarks to these girls. They tried to grab their flowers away from them, and one man stuck his foot out... [A girl] was tripped but did not fall because the crowd was too dense. There were two policemen standing together that were egging on the crowd to jeer, and they themselves were making remarks to us and jeering... None of us complained. I simply told the young girls to keep out of their way. I was just as much alarmed at those policemen as I was at the crowd. ❞

THE SPANISH FLU PANDEMIC

▲ Wearing masks for protection against the virus, Red Cross nurses in Washington, DC, move a patient with Spanish Flu into a quarantine ward.

In early 1918 a deadly virus appeared in North America and Europe. Its effects were kept quiet in the nations fighting in World War I. It was first reported in Spain, which did not fight in the war, so it was named Spanish Flu. The influenza affected mainly young people, and could cause death within twelve hours. By the time the virus died out late in 1920, it had killed more people than had died in conflict during World War I. Between forty million and fifty million people died around the world.

Roy Grist was a doctor at Camp Devens, Massachusetts, a military base near Boston. On September 29, 1918, he wrote a friend describing the appearance of a new type of influenza:

> **"** These men start with what appears to be an attack of la grippe or influenza, and when brought to the hospital they very rapidly develop the most viscous type of pneumonia that has ever been seen. Two hours after admission they have the mahogany spots over the cheek bones, and a few hours later you can begin to see the cyanosis [discoloration] extending from their ears and spreading all over the face, until it is hard to distinguish the colored men from the white. It is only a matter of a few hours then until death comes, and it is simply a struggle for air until they suffocate. It is horrible. We have been averaging about 100 deaths per day, and still keeping it up. **"**

SOURCE EXPLORED

This ward for victims of Spanish Flu was set up in Oakland, California, in 1918. The disease had first appeared in the United States that January. More than one in four Americans got sick and up to 675,000 died. Schools and theaters were closed to prevent the spread of the disease. People wore masks over their mouths when they were out in public. Those suffering from the virus were often placed into quarantine to avoid them infecting others. The virus spread widely around the world, however. It may have been partly spread by soldiers returning home from the Western Front in Europe. The virus finally disappeared quite suddenly from the United States in March 1919. The last global case was recorded in 1920.

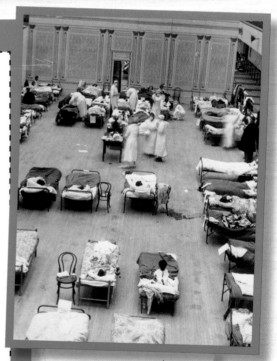

▲ This temporary ward was set up in Oakland Municipal Auditorium. It was staffed by volunteer nurses from the American Red Cross.

THE GROWTH OF EXTREMISM

The end of World War I left much of Europe in turmoil. In Germany, street battles broke out as communists and their right-wing opponents fought for power. An army veteran named Adolf Hitler took charge of a tiny political group, later known as the National Socialist German Workers' Party (NSDAP), or Nazis. In Italy, journalist Benito Mussolini formed the right-wing Fascist Party to appeal to the country's unemployed youth.

▼ *Benito Mussolini (center, with hands on hips) poses with members of his Blackshirts during the March on Rome in 1922. The Blackshirts were a paramilitary group that used violence to intimidate their opponents.*

◀ *Käthe Kollwitz was a leading German artist of the early twentieth century. Her international reputation helped protect her from the Nazis, even though they threatened her with imprisonment for her left-wing political views.*

SOURCE EXPLORED

This dramatic 1920 woodcut by the German artist Käthe Kollwitz, *The Living to the Dead*, shows mourners paying their respects to Karl Liebknecht. Liebknecht had cofounded the communist Spartacus League with Rosa Luxemburg at the end of 1914. After the end of the war, Liebknecht declared the Free German Socialist Republic in Berlin. In January 1919 he helped found the Communist Party of Germany and led an armed uprising in Berlin. Liebknecht and Luxemburg were captured and murdered on January 15 by the Freikorps, right-wing paramilitary units formed of World War I veterans. Their murders ended the possibility of a communist revolution in Germany.

MARCH ON ROME

Although Italy was one of the victors in World War I, the conflict left the country's economy in ruins. Italians also felt poorly rewarded by the peace treaty for their role in the war. Benito Mussolini's promise to return Italy to the glory of ancient Rome drew popular support. In October 1922, Mussolini declared that if his Fascist Party was not put in control of Italy his men—the Blackshirts—would march on the capital in Rome and seize power. His threat persuaded the king and prime minister to hand Mussolini control. Mussolini initially governed constitutionally, but in 1925 he declared himself dictator. The Fascist dictatorship lasted until 1944.

THE GREAT DEPRESSION

While Europe's economies tried to recover from World War I, in the late 1920s the US economy slowed down, resulting in the Wall Street Crash of October 1929. Businesses stopped manufacturing, and many workers lost their jobs. With foreign imports limited in the United States, and with US companies no longer buying supplies, the economic effects led to a worldwide depression. In Chile, for example, mines shut when US firms stopped buying copper. In Europe, the effects of the Great Depression hit even victors such as Britain. In industrial areas in the north, unemployment rates reached 70 percent.

◀ Unemployed shipyard workers from Jarrow in northern England march to London to protest the lack of work in October 1936.

◀ *Unemployed workers became a familiar sight in many US cities during the early 1930s.*

SOURCE EXPLORED

This photograph was taken by Mark Barry in 1934, at the height of the Great Depression in the United States. It shows unemployed workers on benches at the edge of a park in Haddon Heights, New Jersey. Their poses seem to suggest the despair many Americans felt about being unable to work or provide for their families. When the Depression was at its worst, in 1933, about one-quarter of all American workers had no job. Many people moved from the country to the city to try to find work, or headed west to look for work on the West Coast. The worst effects of the Depression were reduced when the government of Franklin D. Roosevelt introduced programs of public works to provide jobs. However, full employment did not return until the outbreak of World War II.

AS THEY SAW IT

" We were a gentle crowd. They were fathers, eighty percent of them. They had held jobs and didn't want to kick society to pieces. They just wanted to go to work and they just couldn't understand. These fellas always had faith that the job was gonna mature, somehow. More and more men were after fewer and fewer jobs. So San Francisco just ground to a halt. Nothing was moving. "

—Ed Paulson recalls the men he met while searching for work in San Francisco in 1931.

HITLER'S RISE

▲ *Thousands of members of the Nazi Party gather during a huge display at one of the annual Nuremberg Rallies.*

Adolf Hitler became leader of the German Workers' Party in 1921 and renamed it the National Socialist German Workers' Party, or Nazis. Imprisoned after an attempt to seize power in Munich in 1923, he wrote *Mein Kampf*, a summary of his political views. He blamed Germany's defeat in World War I on an international conspiracy by Jews and betrayal by left-wing civilian politicians. He argued that Germany should reject the Treaty of Versailles. With unemployment in Germany at 30 percent, Hitler's aggressive message was attractive to many Germans. A powerful public speaker, Hitler began to gain electoral success in the late 1920s.

▼ *Nazi propaganda presented Hitler as offering hope to Germans who resented the country's treatment by the Allies after World War I.*

Unsere letzte Hoffnung: HITLER

NUREMBERG RALLIES

Between 1923 and 1938, the Nazi Party held rallies at least once a year in Nuremberg in southern Germany. From 1927 onwards, they took place in an arena designed by the architect Albert Speer. The rallies were designed to show the power of the Nazi Party. They included marches of thousands of Nazis in militaristic uniforms carrying banners of the swastika symbol the party had adopted. There was militaristic music and fireworks displays, and speeches by Hitler and other party leaders. Huge crowds attended, including children wearing the uniform of the party's youth movement, the Hitler Youth.

SOURCE EXPLORED

This poster for Germany's presidential election in 1932 shows unemployed Germans with the slogan, "Hitler: Our Last Hope." Hitler put Joseph Goebbels in charge of conveying the Nazi message that Germany should reject the terms of the Treaty of Versailles. Goebbels hired the artist Hans Schweitzer to produce Nazi propaganda posters like this one. Hitler and Goebbels reduced the Nazi message to a series of simple slogans that increasingly appealed to Germans as the effects of the Depression worsened after 1930. Nazi support grew, and in the 1932 German election Hitler finished second. In January 1933, however, the president and chancellor of Germany asked for Nazi support to keep their government in power. Hitler agreed—as long as he himself was made chancellor. The deal was agreed upon, but as soon as Hitler took power in January 1933 he began to take control as a dictator.

JAPAN'S WAR ON CHINA

In East Asia, Japan was eager to expand its territory to gain resources. In 1931, the Japanese army had invaded Manchuria in northern China. In 1937, Japanese forces took advantage of fighting between China's Nationalists and Communists to invade the heart of the country. The Chinese united to fight back, beginning a brutal war that lasted until Japan's defeat at the end of World War II (1939–1945).

▼ *Japanese troops march Chinese prisoners into captivity after the invasion of 1937. Most Chinese prisoners were treated badly.*

SOURCE EXPLORED

This photograph shows Chinese refugees. The brutality of the Japanese occupiers forced up to thirty million Chinese to flee their homes to avoid mistreatment. During the so-called "Rape of Nanking," Japanese soldiers committed many atrocities. They held competitions to see who could behead the most Chinese prisoners and they used prisoners for bayonet practice. They buried Chinese men alive and murdered women, children, and even babies.

▲ Millions of Chinese refugees lived in crowded camps in territory that was still under Chinese control.

In December 1937 Japanese forces captured the Chinese capital, Nanking. They killed some three hundred thousand men, women, and children. The German businessman John Rabe lived in Nanking. This is his diary entry for December 13, 1937:

❝ We come across corpses every 100 to 200 yards. The bodies of civilians that I examined had bullet holes in their backs. These people had presumably been fleeing and were shot from behind. The Japanese march through the city in groups of ten to twenty soldiers and loot the shops. If I had not seen it with my own eyes I would not have believed it. They smash open windows and doors and take whatever they like. Allegedly because they're short of rations. I watched with my own eyes as they looted the cafe of our German baker Herr Kiessling.... Some Japanese soldiers dragged their booty away in crates, others requisitioned [took] rickshaws to transport their stolen goods to safety. ❞

WORLD WAR II

In September 1939, Germany invaded Poland. It was the latest move by Adolf Hitler to increase German territory in Europe. This time, however, Britain and France declared war on Germany. By 1940, Hitler had conquered most of Europe—only Britain avoided defeat. By the end of 1941, Hitler had invaded the Soviet Union and the United States had entered the war after Germany's ally, Japan, bombed the US naval base at Pearl Harbor. After their initial successes, by 1944 Germany and Japan were being pushed back. Germany was defeated in May 1945. Japan surrendered in August. Nearly fifty million people died.

◄ This poster was created to encourage Americans to lend money for the war effort. It shows US Marines raising the flag on Iwo Jima as they advanced across the Pacific.

Glen Michael Holtz was a radio operator on a US B-24 Liberator bomber. He flew more than thirty missions over Germany in the last year of the war. Here he remembers a raid early in 1945:

" I descend to the lower flight deck next to the bomb-bay door lever and crouch next to the bomb doors. The call comes over the intercom, 'Open bomb doors,' and I press the lever. The four big doors roll up the sides of the plane like the lids of roll-top desks. All I can see below are clouds. The radar operator is in direct contact with the bombardier; I hear his voice as the radar operator gives instructions to the bombardier. The bombardier is making cruise corrections—flying the plane with his control. The radar operator stays steady and clear on his directions. I hear him say, 'Steady now,' and his next words are 'Bombs away!' I feel the plane lurch upward, then I verify all bombs have been dropped and reach for the door lever. "

SOURCE EXPLORED

In this image, Allied bombs fall on the German city of Dresden in February 1945. After the end of the Blitz, the British began their own bombing campaign against German cities. They were later joined by US aircraft. As German bombing had done in British cities, the Allied bombing not only damaged factories and other war facilities. It also destroyed homes and killed many thousands of civilians. The raid on Dresden from February 13 to 15, 1945, was the most devastating single attack. As many as twenty-five thousand civilians died when blazes started by the bombs were fanned by the wind into a huge firestorm.

▲ From February 13 to February 15, 1,249 British and US bombers launched four raids on Dresden. They dropped incendiary bombs intended to start fires on the ground.

THE PARTITION OF INDIA

▲ A Muslim family sets out with their belongings to move to Pakistan. The new Muslim country was created in two parts: East and West Pakistan. East Pakistan is now known as Bangladesh.

Britain had ruled India since 1763, but many Indians wanted independence. In 1930, the lawyer Mohandas Ghandi (later known as Mahatma, or "Great Soul") began a campaign of civil disobedience against British rule. Eventually, however, it was the cost of governing India that convinced Britain to give up its colony. At midnight on August 14, 1947, British rule ended. India was split into two new nations: India and Pakistan.

The Hindustan Times *reports the end of British rule, but also announces that the British Viceroy, Lord Mountbatten, will become Governor General. India remained in the British Commonwealth, and the governor general represented the Queen.*

SOURCE EXPLORED

The front page of the English language *Hindustan Times* of August 15, 1947, announces India's independence. The paper had been founded in 1924 to support calls for independence. Despite its celebratory tone, however, the partition of India was a human disaster. Under the terms of independence, Pakistan was to become a Muslim majority country while India remained a Hindu majority country. This led to one of the largest human migrations in history. Millions of Muslims traveled to West and East Pakistan (modern-day Bangladesh) while millions of Hindus and Sikhs went south to India. By the end of 1948, more than fifteen million people had moved. Up to two million more had died in violence that broke out between the two groups.

AS THEY SAW IT

66 When the dawn came—I cannot describe to you how heady the feeling was. It was as though everything was new. The world was new. The trees were greener. ... It was too fantastic. You felt you could do anything, now that we were free. 99

—Schoolgirl Birenda Kaur reflects on the excitement of independence before the violence began.

ASSASSINATION OF GANDHI

The leader of India's Independence movement, Mahatma Gandhi, was born into a wealthy family but faced racial prejudice while working as a lawyer in South Africa. He became politically active and when he returned to India he devoted his life to gaining independence from British rule through nonviolent civil disobedience. After independence, however, Gandhi's tolerance of the Muslims who still lived in India angered extremist Hindus. One shot him dead in New Delhi on January 30, 1948.

◄ Gandhi's followers gather his ashes after his cremation on the banks of the Jumna River, which is sacred to Hindus. A million mourners attended Gandhi's funeral.

▼ Gandhi's simple dress was a symbol linking him to India's poorest peasants. He believed that to wear other clothes to meet world leaders would be "disrespectful."

AS THEY SAW IT

❝ Just as he climbed the raised lawn to reach his seat for the prayer, a gunshot was heard ... Barely seconds later, when another shot pierced the air, I knew by instinct what had happened. As I turned my eyes, I saw the man pull the trigger for the third time ... In a moment Gandhiji fell ... [A little later] I saw somebody had put up twigs in a circle around the spot [where] his body fell and even lit a candle. ❞

–Journalist K. D. Madan recalls the moment Gandhi was shot by Nathuram Godse on January 30, 1948.

SOURCE EXPLORED

In this photograph, Gandhi smiles broadly. He wears round wire-rimmed spectacles and his trademark garment, the *dhoti*. The dhoti was the traditional dress of the poorest Indians, and Gandhi wore it as a symbol of simplicity and poverty. Gandhi himself spun the cotton to make the garment. On his feet he wore leather *chappels,* or sandals, as a sign of India's self-sufficiency. Gandhi dressed this way every day from 1921 until his death. He developed his policy of nonviolence during the 1920s and 1930s, when he tried to break down barriers between India's Hindus and Muslims. In 1930, he led a "Salt March" to protest the British tax on salt. The British imprisoned him many times for civil disobedience. After partition, Gandhi worked hard to stop Hindus and Muslims massacring each other. His perceived sympathy toward Muslims led to his murder by a Hindu extremist in New Delhi on January 30, 1948.

CREATION OF ISRAEL

▲ David Ben-Gurion (left), the leader of the Jewish settlers in Palestine, signs the declaration creating the State of Israel in Tel Aviv on May 14, 1948.

In the late nineteenth century, Jews began arguing for the creation of a Jewish homeland in Palestine. Jews began moving to what was then an Arab-occupied part of the Ottoman Empire. After some six million European Jews died in the Holocaust in World War II, the United Nations (UN) agreed to create a Jewish state in Palestine. On May 14, 1948, Jewish leaders declared the creation of the state of Israel. The decision remains highly controversial. Some Arab states still refuse to acknowledge Israel's right to exist.

SOURCE EXPLORED

If it were not for the abandoned cars in this photograph from 1948, the image could be straight out of The Bible. The image shows Palestinians fleeing on foot as a result of the United Nations Partition Plan, under which much of Palestine was to be given to the Jews for their new state. A civil war had broken out in the region as soon as the UN plan was adopted in November 1947. The Palestinian exodus of 1948 (known in Arabic as the "Nakba," which means disaster or catastrophe) saw as many as 700,000 Palestinian Arabs leave Palestine. Jewish leaders argued that they left voluntarily and could have stayed. A further 160,000 Palestinians became "internal refugees," meaning that they now lived in the Jewish state of Israel.

ARAB/ISRAELI WARS

The day after the creation of Israel was declared, May 15, 1948, the new state was invaded by troops from its Arab neighbors, Egypt, Syria, and Jordan. After ten months of fighting, Israel was victorious. The peace settlement left it in control not only of the area laid out in the UN plan but also 60 percent of the land designated for Palestinians. In June 1967, the two sides fought again in the Six-Day War. Another Israeli victory brought more Palestinian territory under Israeli rule. These areas are now known as the Occupied Territories.

▼ Arab refugees make their way out of Palestine. Most of the Arabs who left moved to Lebanon, Syria, and Jordan.

CHINA'S CIVIL WAR

In China, the warring Communists and Nationalists had united to fight the Japanese invasion in 1937. After Japan's defeat in World War II, the Nationalists regained control of the Chinese government. In July 1946, the pre-war civil war with the Communists resumed. Led by Mao Zedong, the Communists attracted support through policies such as placing land in communal ownership. When Manchuria fell to the Communists in January 1949, many Nationalists surrendered. Mao's troops marched into Beijing, where he declared the creation of the People's Republic of China on October 1, 1949. Two million Nationalists fled to the island of Taiwan, where they established the Republic of China.

◀ Communist soldiers march beneath an arch in the Great Wall of China during their triumphant campaign in 1949.

◄ Mao Zedong addresses his followers. His teachings were particularly popular among China's millions of peasants and urban poor.

SOURCE EXPLORED

This photograph shows Mao Zedong addressing his supporters in 1944. Born into a peasant family in 1893, Mao became a teacher and joined the Chinese Communist Party when it was created in 1921. In 1927, Mao led a group of Communists to the mountains in his home province to escape the ruling Nationalists. There, he plotted a peasant revolution based on the beliefs of Marx and Lenin. Mao took control of the Communist Party after the Long March of 1935, when he led the Red Army to a remote region of China for safety. Only some eight thousand of the one hundred thousand communists who set out survived. For nearly fifteen years Mao fought a guerrilla war against the Nationalists, apart from the period when he cooperated with them against the Japanese. The Communists finally emerged victorious in 1949.

AS THEY SAW IT

" When the Communist armies came in, the people lined the streets offering them hot tea in glasses, as they do in hot weather, but the soldiers refused to take anything, not even the tea. And the Communist soldiers were .... holding hands and dancing in circles as they came down the main street. And behind them came the tanks and armored cars. And it was really a joyful occasion. "

—Norman Watts, an English businessman, describes the arrival of the Communists in Shanghai in the summer of 1949.

THE COLD WAR

▲ US artillery fires during the Korean War (1950–1953), the first armed conflict of the Cold War. The United States and its allies defeated a communist attempt to seize Korea.

After World War II, the United States and the Soviet Union were the world's only global superpowers. The world divided as states allied themselves with either the free-market United States or the communist Soviet Union. For the next forty years, the ideological divide between the capitalist West and the communist East created a period of huge international tension known as the "Cold War." The two superpowers did not fight directly. Instead they tried to build up their international political influence by supporting their respective allies.

◀ *The hammer and sickle on this soldier's shoulders shows that he is an officer in the Soviet Red Army. The image suggests that the creation of NATO has frustrated Soviet aggression against the West.*

SOURCE EXPLORED

This 1949 US cartoon shows a menacing Soviet soldier looking across the sea to the West. Above the West flies a giant flag reading "North Atlantic Pact." The flag is a reference to the formation of the North Atlantic Treaty Organization, or NATO, on April 4, 1949. NATO was an alliance of Western nations—including the United States, Great Britain, France, and other European countries—that were committed to help one another in the event of Soviet aggression toward any of them. Its formation reflected the very real fear in the West of a Soviet attack. NATO also aimed to ensure European unity after the devastation of World War II, which had killed some 36.5 million Europeans. For their part, the Soviets saw the creation of NATO as an aggressive move by the United States and its allies. In response, they formed a similar organization with their own allies in 1955, the Warsaw Pact.

THE BERLIN WALL

At the end of World War II, the German capital of Berlin was divided into zones run by the Americans, British, French, and Soviets. The city was inside Soviet-controlled East Germany, however, and many East Germans escaped to the West via Berlin. Overnight on August 12–13, 1961, East German soldiers erected a barrier across the city to separate the Soviet zone from the Western zones.

▼ *A young East Berliner cements concrete blocks to help build a wall to strengthen the temporary barriers originally erected across Berlin.*

▲ *A young West German boy climbs on the Berlin Wall. In the early months of the wall's existence, friends and families gathered to shout messages across it.*

SOURCE EXPLORED

A young West Berliner plays on the Berlin Wall. In East Berlin, such games could end in death. The purpose of the wall was to prevent East Germans from fleeing to the West, and around two hundred people were shot while attempting to cross the wall. Some five thousand people did escape, but most of those escapes came soon after the original barrier was built. Later, escape became almost impossible. The East Germans replaced the original barrier with two high walls topped by barbed wire and separated by a no-man's land that was patrolled by soldiers with dogs. Guards kept watch from towers.

East Berlin schoolboy Jan-Aart de Rooij was fourteen years old when the Berlin Wall was built. At the time he was staying at a camp in West Germany. On his return to Berlin he decided to stay in the West. Here he describes the later building of the wall as seen from West Berlin:

66 There was this one street we used to go to which was split down the middle by the wall. The street was in the west but the houses were in the east. The soldiers bricked up the front doors but people jumped out of the windows. There was a group of us on the western side who used to all try to knock off the top level of the wall before the cement had time to dry. We were a bit of a mob; we would all surge together and smash it. It was a very addictive game. 99

THE VIETNAM WAR

The Vietnam War was the most serious military conflict of the Cold War. It began in the 1950s, when communists supported by China created North Vietnam. In the early 1960s, US troops arrived to support South Vietnam against communist aggression. Although growing numbers of American, Australian, and New Zealand troops arrived, South Vietnam was ultimately defeated in 1975. The communists' guerrilla tactics proved more effective than the conventional military tactics of the Americans and their allies.

◄ A Viet Cong guerrilla guards the entrance to a tunnel complex. The Viet Cong could live underground for weeks at a time to evade US forces.

◄ *Fire trucks rush to the site of an explosion in Saigon during the Tet Offensive on January 30, 1968. All the major cities of South Vietnam came under attack.*

SOURCE EXPLORED

This photograph shows the moment after a bomb detonates in the South Vietnamese capital, Saigon, during the Tet Offensive of January 30, 1968. The North Vietnamese fought the war in part by supplying guerrilla fighters in South Vietnam, known as the Viet Cong. During the New Year holiday, or Tet, Viet Cong and North Vietnamese troops launched simultaneous surprise attacks on many South Vietnamese cities. Caught off guard, US and South Vietnamese troops fought back, inflicting heavy losses on the attackers. Images like this shocked Americans by demonstrating the vast resources and manpower of the enemy. Many Americans began to believe that the United States could not win the war, hastening America's exit from Vietnam.

AS THEY SAW IT

" Cutting the roads was a superhuman task. Our only tools were picks, shovels, and saws. When trees were too big to cut down by hand we blew them down with dynamite. It took at least twenty people to roll the big trees aside ... Most of the time we worked only at night because that's when the trucks and soldiers came and we needed to be ready to help if they got stuck ... Life in the jungle was extremely hard. When we weren't supplied with rice we ate whatever we could find ... Sometimes we had to scrape fungus and moss off rocks to eat. "

—Schoolgirl Vu Thi Vinh recalls building the "Ho Chi Minh Trail," a secret path by which North Vietnam sent supplies to the Viet Cong.

THE FALL OF COMMUNISM

▲ A Berliner hammers pieces off the Berlin Wall as souvenirs in November 1989. Crowds flocked to the wall after East German border guards abandoned their posts.

For forty years after World War II, the Soviet Union maintained its control of Eastern Europe, despite local uprisings in Hungary, Czechoslovakia, and Poland. In 1985, however, Mikhail Gorbachev became leader of the Soviet Union. Gorbachev believed that the cost of the Cold War was crippling the Soviet economy. He set out to improve relations between East and West. The process he began ended in 1989 with the collapse of communist rule across Europe.

◀ *Ronald Reagan and Mikhail Gorbachev agree to a treaty limiting medium-range nuclear missiles in Washington, DC, in December 1987. The good relationship between the two men helped speed up the end of the Cold War as the Soviet Union became more open and less hostile toward the West.*

RETURN TO DEMOCRACY

Throughout Eastern Europe, citizens saw the collapse of the Soviet Union as a chance to overthrow their communist governments. In Czechoslovakia's so-called "Velvet Revolution," mass protests brought down the government in December 1989. Poland, Hungary, and Bulgaria made the transition to democracy peacefully in the early 1990s. In October 1990 West and East Germany were formally reunified. The only violence came in Romania, where the dictator, Nicolae Ceausescu, was overthrown and executed.

SOURCE EXPLORED

US President Ronald Reagan shakes the hand of the General Secretary of the Soviet Communist Party Mikhail Gorbachev on December 8, 1987, after signing an historic agreement to limit nuclear weapons. A year earlier, Gorbachev had surprised the West when he called for all nations to get rid of their nuclear weapons by 2000. In reality, Gorbachev knew the Soviet Union could not afford to keep up an arms race against the United States. The end of the nuclear threat was a sign that the Cold War was over. Russia could no longer afford to maintain its communist empire. Without Soviet backing, the East Germans allowed the Berlin Wall to fall in November 1989. Over the next months one communist country after another declared its independence from Russia.

ISLAMIC EXTREMISM

On September 11, 2001, Islamic terrorists flew airliners into buildings in New York and Washington, DC. The 9/11 attacks were a sign of a new world threat from Islamic extremists.

US President George W. Bush declared a "War on Terror" in September 2001 to punish those responsible for the attacks. That conflict has since involved wars against Islamic forces in Afghanistan, Iraq, Yemen, and other countries, while terrorist attacks have occurred around the world.

◀ Rescue workers and reporters stand amid wreckage near Ground Zero in New York City, where airliners demolished the towers of the World Trade Center on 9/11, killing more than two thousand people.

◀ *A sniper sights his rifle as his colleagues survey a village in Afghanistan. Because extremists mix with the regular population, it takes reliable intelligence to be able to tell the two apart.*

SOURCE EXPLORED

US soldiers from Fourth Infantry Regiment survey a village in Afghanistan during a patrol in February 2009. Western troops invaded Afghanistan in October 2001 to overthrow the Islamic Taliban government, which supported the al-Qaeda terrorist group. In March 2003 Western troops invaded Iraq to bring down the dictator Saddam Hussein. Conflict continues in both countries today. Western forces have had to adapt their tactics to fight a new type of warfare against enemies who often wear civilian clothing and hide among innocent citizens. The terrorists use homemade improvised weapons or blow themselves up as suicide bombers, believing they will go to Paradise. In such a conflict, intelligence is often the only way to stop extremist attacks before they happen. Armed with intelligence, Western forces use unmanned drones to destroy enemy targets from the air.

AS THEY SAW IT

" The Muslims came to our home and asked us whether we would continue to believe in Christ or turn and believe in Mohammed. We told them that we would always believe in Christ. They then stabbed Ayodele, pushed him out of the house all the while asking him whether he still believed in Christ. The young man repeatedly answered them that he would never deny his Lord and then they hacked him to death. "

—A schoolgirl describes the murder of her brother by Islamist terrorists in northern Nigeria in June 2000.

TIMELINE

1914	**June 28:** The Austrian archduke Franz Ferdinand is assassinated in Sarajevo. His death triggers a series of declarations of war that eventually draws most countries in Europe into World War I.
1917	**November 6–7:** In the October Revolution, Bolsheviks led by Vladimir Lenin overthrow the government in Russia.
1918	**February 6:** The first British women are given the right to vote. Spanish Influenza appears in North America and Europe. In the next two years it will kill up to fifty million people worldwide.
	November 11: World War I ends in an armistice.
1919	**June 28:** The Treaty of Versailles is signed in Paris.
1920	**January 10:** The League of Nations is created as a body to avoid conflicts by settling international disputes through diplomacy.
1922	**October 22:** Benito Mussolini, leader of the Fascist Party in Italy, stages a March on Rome in a successful attempt to have himself appointed the country's prime minister.
	December 30: Lenin creates the Union of Soviet Socialist Republics, or the Soviet Union.
1923	After a failed attempt to seize power in Munich, Adolf Hitler is sent to prison, where he writes a summary of his beliefs, Mein Kampf.
1925	Mussolini becomes the dictator of Italy.
1929	**October 29:** The Wall Street Crash heralds a slowdown in world trade that contributes to the coming of the Great Depression.
1933	**April 27:** Adolf Hitler is made chancellor of Germany in return for supporting the then government.
1937	**July 7:** Japanese forces invade China, beginning the Second Sino–Japanese War, which lasts until 1945.
1939	**September 1:** Germany's invasion of Poland triggers the start of World War II in Europe.
1941	**June 22:** Germany invades the Soviet Union.
	December 11: The United States enters the war after Japan bombs the base of the US Pacific Fleet at Pearl Harbor, Hawaii.
1945	**May 8:** The war in Europe ends with Germany's surrender. Soviet troops occupy much of Eastern Europe.

1945	*August 15:* Japan surrenders after two atomic bombs are dropped on the cities of Hiroshima and Nagasaki.
1947	*August 14–15:* At midnight British rule ends in India, which becomes two states, India and Pakistan.
1948	*January 30:* Indian leader Mahatma Gandhi is assassinated.
	May 14: The State of Israel is created; it is immediately attacked by its Arab neighbors.
1949	*April 4:* The United States and its allies create the North Atlantic Treaty Organization, or NATO.
	October 1: Mao Zedong proclaims the creation of the People's Republic of China after a civil war against China's Nationalists.
1950	*June 25:* The Korean War begins as communists try to take over the country. When peace is declared in 1953, Korea is divided into the communist North and the democratic South.
1955	*May 14:* The Soviet Union and its allies create the Warsaw Pact.
1961	*August 12–13:* Overnight East German authorities create a barrier dividing Berlin. It is later built into a strong wall.
1965	*March 8:* The first US ground forces arrive to join the civil war in Vietnam.
1973	*March 29:* The last US forces leave Vietnam. South Vietnam is defeated in April 1975.
1985	*March 14:* Mikhail Gorbachev becomes leader of the Soviet Union and begins improving relations with the West.
1989	*November 9:* The Berlin Wall is opened. *December:* In Eastern Europe, citizens in a series of countries begin to overthrow their communist governments.
2001	*September 9:* Islamic terrorist attacks on North America kill 2,977 people.
	October 7: A US-led coalition invades Afghanistan to topple the Islamic Taliban government.
2003	*March 20:* An international coalition, or alliance, invades Iraq to overthrow the dictator Saddam Hussein.

GLOSSARY

abdicate For a monarch to give up his or her throne.

armistice A halt in a conflict.

arms race A competition between nations to develop better weapons.

assassination A murder committed for a political reason.

civil disobedience A refusal to obey unjust laws, as a form of protest.

colony A country or area that is controlled by another country.

communists People who believe that property should be shared among everyone and that economic activity should be directed by the goverment.

constitutionally According to the constitution of a country.

Depression A long slump in economic activity such as trade.

dictator A ruler with total power over a country.

extremism The holding of extreme political or religious views.

fascist Someone who believes society should be organized in an ordered, militaristic way, with few individual rights.

guerrilla A fighter who carries out irregular actions, such as ambushes, against a larger enemy force.

Hindu A follower of the ancient religion of India.

Holocaust The Nazis' mass murder of Jews and others in World War II.

hunger strike A prolonged refusal to eat carried out as a protest.

intelligence In military terms, useful information about the enemy.

Islamic Related to Islam, the religion followed by Muslims.

morale The belief an individual or group has that they will succeed in a particular task.

Muslim A follower of Islam.

neutrality The state of not taking sides in a dispute or war.

pandemic Describes a disease that affects a large area and many people.

paramilitary Civilians organized in the same way as a military force.

quarantine A place where sick people are kept in isolation to prevent their sickness being passed on.

reparations Financial payments made by a country to compensate for damage caused by a war.

right wing Describes conservative political beliefs.

socialist Someone who believes in a system in which economic activity is directed by the government.

suffrage The right to vote in political elections.

swastika A cross with broken arms, used as a symbol by the Nazis.

virus A microorganism that infects living creatures with sickness.

FURTHER INFORMATION

Books

Brezina, Corona. *The Treaty of Versailles, 1919: A Primary Source Examination of the Treaty that Ended World War I.* Primary Sources of American Treaties. New York: Rosen Central, 2006.

Burgan, Michael. *The Berlin Wall: Barrier to Freedom.* Snapshots in History. Minneapolis, MN: Compass Point Books, 2007.

George, Enzo. *World War I: The War to End All Wars. Voices of War.* New York: Cavendish Square, 2014.

Harkins, Susan Hale, and William H. Harkins. *The Fall of the Soviet Union, 1991.* Monumental Milestones: Great Events of Modern Times. Hockessin, DE: Mitchell Lane Publishers, 2007.

Hillstrom, Kevin. *The Cold War.* Primary Sourcebook. Detroit: Omnigraphics, 2006.

Malaspina, Ann. *Mao Zedong and the Chinese Revolution.* New York: Enslow Publishers, 2016.

Rau, Dana Meachen. *Who Was Gandhi?* Who Was. New York: Turtleback, 2014.

Websites

www.history1900s.about.com/od/timelines/tp/timeline.htm
Decade-by-decade timelines of the twentieth century from About.com.

www.history-world.org/great_depression.htm
History World page on the Great Depression around the world.

www.mrdowling.com/706-hitler.html
An account of Adolf Hitler's rise to power from MrDowling.com.

www.ducksters.com/history/world_war_ii/
A Ducksters page with links to pages on all aspects of World War II.

Publisher's note to educators and parents: Our editors have carefully reviewed these websites to ensure that they are suitable for students. Many websites change frequently, however, and we cannot guarantee that a site's future contents will continue to meet our high standards of quality and educational value. Be advised that students should be closely supervised whenever they access the Internet.

INDEX

3/ 36